EVERY FREAKING! DAY

WITH RACHELL RAY

ALSO BY ELIZABETH HILTS:

Getting In Touch With Your Inner Bitch

EVERY FREAKING! DAY WITH RACHELL RAY

ELIZABETH HILTS

GRAND CENTRAL
PUBLISHING

NEW YORK   BOSTON

Grand Central Publishing
Hachette Book Group USA
237 Park Avenue
New York, NY 10017

Visit our website at www.HachetteBookGroupUSA.com

Printed in the United States of America

First Edition: September 2008

Grand Central Publishing is a division of Hachette Book Group USA, Inc.
The Grand Central Publishing name and logo is a trademark of Hachette
Book Group USA, Inc.
10 9 8 7 6 5 4 3 2 1

Book design by Laura D. Campbell

Photography by Neil Swanson

Book production by Tom Connor & Elizabeth Hilts

LCCN: 2008921962

ISBN-10: 0-446-509442
ISBN-13: 978-0-446-50944-2

EVERY FREAKING! DAY
WITH RACHELL RAY

PARODY

11

in every freaking! issue

READY, SET, DONE!
tools, tricks and techniques to get it over with

17

14

ON THE COVER

Photography by Neil Swanson
Makeup by Dawn Collins
Hair by Shannon Hector
Wardrobe/styling by Elizabeth Hilts
Food by Elizabeth Hilts
Production by Tom Connor & Elizabeth Hilts
Design by Laura Campbell

FREAKING!
EVERY DAY
WITH RACHELL RAY
PARODY

Oh My Buns!
Burgers of the Month

No Time, No Sweat!
30-SECOND MEALS

(Minor) Celeb Fridge
with Paula Deane

EZ ENTERTAINING
for Lay-Z-Daze

SWELL Wines under
SWILL $5.99

10,081 Recipes

Hey, you!
It's me! Again!
Want to do a shout
out to my crew.

12

EVERY FREAKING! DAY
WITH RACHELL RAY

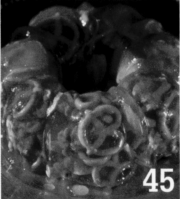

Hey, You!

Welcome to my magazine, *Every Freaking! Day with Rachell Ray!* I'm Rachell Ray and I cook 30-minute meals—that's meals that you can make really quick, like in 30 minutes—every freaking day.

Of course you should take that "30-minute" thing with a grain or two of salt—which I LOVE! Some of the recipes take a little longer, but you know what? It doesn't matter because it's all just marketing, for chrissakes and "30-minute meals" sounds better than 45-minute meals or 90-minute meals or whatever.

Anywhoooo…

You know what I love the most about *Every Freaking! Day with Rachell Ray?* EVERYTHING! This issue is all about making Every Freaking Day a celebration, so it's crammed with quick and easy recipes, great ideas you can totally entertain with, and a whole mess of other interesting stuff.

PLUS, you're invited to my family reunion dinner party! I can't wait to show you all the kooky-zany stuff that went on at that event! What's not to love, right?

Love,

I'm a cook, not a baker, which is one reason I cooked up this no-bake chocolate cake! Look for the "recipe" in the Yumm-Oh! section.

As a nutritionist and CSI investigator, I feel it's my duty to inform you that the combinations of ingredients in your Celebration Salad with Purple Foxglove Blossoms ["HIT THE DECK!," JUNE] could, in fact, cause anyone who ate it to hit the deck—for keeps! Foxglove is also known as Witches' Gloves, Dead Men's Bells, and is considered poisonous.

— S. SIDLE, *Las Vegas, NV*

Duly noted. My bad. Hey, even I don't get it right every freaking time.

MY MOTHER-IN-LAW BOUGHT ME A GIFT SUBSCRIPTION TO YOUR MAGAZINE and I've tried to cancel about 10 times. What do I need to do to cease delivery? For the love of all things holy, stop! Stop the madness now! Please, I'm begging you!

— G. MAILLE, *Boston, MA*

Glad to hear that you're enjoying your present! Thanks to MIL for helping me help you!

I'd love to know where you got the fabulous bowls for the HOT DIGGITY DAWGS AND BEAN STROUP ["30-SECOND MEALS," FEBRUARY].

— E. SCUDERIA, *Lake George, NY*

I love them, too! Those bowls are $12.98 each at everyfreakingday.com.

MY HUSBAND AND I CAN'T WAIT TO MAKE YOUR HAMMY MAC N' CHEESE (WHIZ) ["BITE THIS!," MAY], but haven't been able to find the ham you used—the 2006 Alba Quercus Reserve. We looked on-line and found a website that's hawking it for $2,100 per leg, which means the 1/4 lb. the recipe calls for would cost $40. Do you have any suggestions for substitute hams that might be a little kinder to our pocketbook?

— A. GIFFORD, *Normal, IL*

Listen, good food can be expensive. Don't you deserve to splurge on the very best sometimes? Easy for me to say, ha ha!

Dear Rach,
Although I am currently living in a "safe place," I appreciate fine foods as much as anyone else and was thrilled to come across your KIDS N' KITTIES RECIPE FOR RIDDLIN PUDDIN in a recent issue. In addition to it being a scrumptious dessert, I was pleasantly surprised to find that I napped quietly for most of the night and bit no one. The dish is now being considered by staff for inclusion in the daily menu!

— JANICE McCLUGGAGE, *Somewhere Upstate*

No biting? Bonus!

Hey, You! Tell us what you think (not what you really think, just what you think we would probably like to think you think). Letters will be edited for profanities and threats, and used in all known media in perpetuity. **letters@everyfreakingday.com**

No-Bake Chocolate Cake

I never met a snack made from chocolate cake, crème filling and "ganache" that I didn't like, and this "layer cake" really piles them on. Super easy to make, just assemble all the ingredients, invite a friend over and share a bottle of wine while you watch them put it together!

- **3 8" foam disks**
- **white glue**
- **2 boxes Ring Dings**
- **2 boxes Yodels**
- **2 boxes Hostess Chocolate Cup Cakes**
- **2 boxes 100-Calorie Pack Chocolate Cupcakes**
- **1 box toothpicks (2000 count)**

Stack and glue disks.

Unwrap your snack cakes.

Attach the cakes to your foam using the toothpicks.

Hello, Mr. Cake! What better way to say, "back off, **I'm totally PMS-ing!**"

Gotta Haves

One way to make sure you can always put a tasty meal on the table in 30 minutes or less is to keep your pantry stocked with the things I call "ingredients"—stuff you pick up at the grocery store or order on-line.

Rachell's Shopping List

A SALT WITH A DEADLY SENSE OF HUMOR

The only thing I love more than EVOO is salt. So my new **RACHELL RAY'S WHEN IT'S RAY'S, IT POURS SALT** was a natural.

MIX IT UP!

I love a tasty cake, I just don't want to make one myself. But that shouldn't stop you from trying my new **RACHELL RAY'S CAN'T BEAT IT WITH A STICK CAKE MIX**

STOCK UP!

You'll want to buy cases of **RACHELL RAY'S CHICKIE WICKIE WACKIE CHICKEN STOCK** for the label alone!

Take 5 (or less) — 30-SECOND FAKEZPACHO

This bogus gazpacho will be ready quicker than you can say "ole!"

1. Open a jar of salsa (I like my food spicy, so I go with extra hot). Empty into a big bowl, mix in the juice of 2 limes, 1 cup water, 1 cup of ice and stir until the ice melts. Serve in smaller bowls.

CENTERPIECE OF THE MONTH

Book This Table!

Flowers—what a waste! And pricey? Ooh, baby! For a cheap centerpiece that's sure to get your guests talking, **just gather up the most interesting books on your shelves** and drop them in the center of the table.

Find even more great Rachell Ray books at **everyfreakingday.com**

What the Hell's This?

Secret Ingredients That'll Really Leave 'Em Guessing.

It's so easy to fall into a rut in the kitchen, cranking out the same old same old. Ya gotta mix it up sometimes or you'll just go nuts (and I'll lose a valuable revenue stream). Here are a few of my latest ideas for faboo variations on conventional snacks, meals and desserts.

Super "Nutty" Kettle Corn

When you cook down anchovies, they end up tasting kinda like salted nuts. So when I was thinking about making sweet and salty popcorn for movie night with my sweetie, it hit me—this is something that will make him wonder, "Oh dear mother in heaven, what has she done this time?" I love messin' with peoples' minds (and stomachs), don't you?

1 jar anchovy fillets (or a tube of anchovy paste)
1 stick unsalted butter
1 bag microwave kettle corn

Combine the butter and anchovies and cook over medium heat until the butter melts and the anchovies dissolve. Meanwhile, prepare the kettle corn. When the corn is popped, pour it into a gigantic bowl. Pour that butter and anchovy mixture over the kettle corn, give it a good mix to distribute all that nutty, salty goodness. Serve and enjoy!

PB&J Smoothie

Hey, the sammie and the milk all end up in the same place, right? This smoothie cuts out the middleman.

1 big clump of smooth peanut butter (eyeball it)

The same amount of your favorite jelly or jam (I'm a grape girl myself)

2 slices soft white bread (you can remove the crusts if you're picky)

Some milk

A couple of ice cubes

Toss your pb, your j and your moo juice into the blender and let 'er rip.

Twisted Strawberry Shortcake

1 box crème-filled shortcakes

1 bag frozen strawberries

Balsamic vinegar

Freshly ground black pepper

1 palmful sugar

1 tub dessert topping

1 glug (or 2 glugs) hot sauce

Cayenne pepper (for garnish)

Remove wrappers from shortcakes and split those puppies down the middle lengthwise. Lay them on a platter.

Mix together the strawberries, sugar and black pepper.

Get your dessert topping into a mixing bowl, add the hot sauce, stir together until the hot sauce is completely incorporated into the dessert topping. It'll be a nice pink color.

Pour the strawberries down on top over the shortcakes. Dollop on your spicy dessert topping, sprinkle on a little cayenne and TA-DAH! it on the plate. I like to bring the hot sauce to the table to add a little heat to mine. So far no one else has been tempted to follow suit.

tip

RR Time Saver:
To cut down on clean-up, forget about utensils and use your hands. After all, they're the best tools you've got, right?

People expect dessert. But they'll never expect this strawberry "shortcake" with the punch of hot sauce and cayenne pepper!

Doin' It My Way

Cooking isn't rocket science, it's cooking. But my editor tells me that my way of doing things confuses some people and she insisted on including "real" measurements and stuff. So here's a glossary to help you interpret what I'm talking about.

Measuring, My Way

I'm not a baker, I'm a cook, so I don't use measuring cups and spoons. Here's what I do instead to make cooking simple and easy.

Slop:
1 palmful

RR Math Tip:
If 1 slop equals 1 palmful, then a 1/2 slop would be about 1/4 cup, a 1/4 slop equals a couple of tablespoons and so on. See? Simple!

Glug:
The amount of liquid that comes out of a bottle when you hold it over an open pan or bowl for the count of 5 (or 1 cup).

Whoa! (formerly "once around the pan"):
I used to think that once around the pan was about 2 tablespoons, but it turns out that it can be as much as 1/2 cup! Who knew? So lately I've been using this term to remind me to "go easy, Rach."

A pound:
Any supermarket container of meat. I'm not responsible for what those butchers are doing so use your brains, people. Obviously, you'll need to adjust the rest of the ingredients in a recipe to accommodate the size of the package.

"Whoops!":
About 1 tsp.

Prep and Cook, My Way

I'm not a chef, I'm a cook, so I don't use a lot of technical terms. Here's how I talk about making cooking simple and easy.

The Official Rachell Ray Garbage Bowl:
The name says it all and it's a real time saver. But you wouldn't believe the amount of shit I get for not keeping the cans and wrappers separate from the food scraps. Something about "compost." If you want to complicate things, be my guest and buy *two* Official Rachell Ray Garbage Bowls (available at everyfreakingday.com).

Chop to it:
Like "hop to it" only with an Official Rachell Ray Knife (available at everyfreakingday.com)

Tina Turner it:
Grab the handle of the pot or pan you're cooking in and give it a brisk shake to move the contents around a bit.

Flaunt it on the plate!:
Transfer a finished dish to a serving platter or individual dish.

The Ritual Burning of the Bread:
Putting bread, buns or rolls under the broiler and forgetting about them until they are charred and nearly catch fire. I do it Every Freaking Time!

Talking, My Way

I'm not a writer, I'm a cook, so I don't use standard English. It's like I'm speaking a whole other language!

EVOO, that's extra virgin olive oil:
Extra virgin olive oil (available at everyfreakingday.com). This is the *ne plus ultra* of Rachellisms, the one that is in the dictionary. Take that, all you haters out there.

Die-licious:
Something that's so good you want to fall over dead on the spot.

K'fork me:
Put a knife and fork in me and call me done.

Bogus:
Anything that tastes like it was really complicated but was, in fact, super easy to make.

Healthtritious:
A dish that's not just healthful, it's nutritious and figure-friendly, too!

Entreetizers:
Entrees that double as appetizers.

Strourp:
It could be a stew, but it's not as thick. It could be a soup, but it's not as thin. It could be a chroup if it has milk and potatoes in it. Why are there two "r's" in there? Hello! RR? Make the connection, people…

Fabulicious:
Fabulous AND delicious.

Look for more Rach-isms at
everyfreakingday.com

EVERY DAY raves

Timing is everything when I'm trying to beat the clock with my 30-minute meals, so I keep plenty of these **TICK TOCK TIMERS** close at hand. $49.98 each at everyfreakingday.com.

I call my double timer **Jimmy Two-Times** after a character in my favorite movie, "The Godfather." Or was it "Goodfellas"?

These groovy **LOOPY LIMONCELLO EARRINGS** remind me of what was in fashion back in the day. $29.95 at everyfreakingday.com (quantities limited).

Hey, kids!

Wish you could check out my latest really fave rave: My fleet of bio-diesel-powered luxury SUVs, but that would be a security risk. I've awarded them the very first Rachell Ray Green Seal of Approval. PLUS, look for my new line of eco-friendly products, coming really soon to everyfreakingday.com/green_seal_of_approval. Meanwhile, check out the 411 on my new home bio-diesel plant that recycles leftover EVOO (details on page 24).

I am such a **CHILE HEAD** and so is this **NECKLACE** that mixes classic pearls with enameled Scotch bonnet peppers that are hot, hotter, hottest! $5,000 at everyfreakingday.com.

EVERY DAY raves

Mama Said, Mama Said

By now everyone knows that my mom is my mom, and she's just adorable. This apple didn't fall far from that tree and when I start to get a little full of myself, I remember all of the great things my mom used to say when I needed a little reminding about how to live right. Because we all need a little push in the right direction now and then, I thought I'd share a little of my mom's wisdom with you.

"Work hard, work in places where you can eat for free, and shut up."

Hey, two outta three ain't bad, Mom!

"Put a little something aside for that rainy day."

I think I've got that one covered...

"When life gives you lemons, trade them for some limes and make a margarita."

That's my mom!

Talk about the booby prize! I found this **CUPCAKE SALT AND PEPPER SHAKER SET** in a junk shop, can you believe that? Here's a tip for ya: If you want to add some fun and funky style to your tabletop, **go shopping!**

Eat your veggies! This **GARDEN FRESH PLATE**—hand-crafted just for me in Italy—is healthy AND figure friendly! **$238.95** set of four at everyfreakingday.com.

Success is 10 percent inspiration, 90 percent perspiration. On those rare occasions when my imagination is running dry, I turn to my collection of **ANTIQUE COOKBOOKS** for that essential dose of motivation. The result? No sweat! Sorry, these babies are strictly **NFS** (that's "not for sale").

"Inspired" Chicken á la Queen

You don't have to invent something new in the kitchen. In fact, there are some people—and I'm talkin' famous chef people, here—who say that the real challenge is getting the classic dishes right. I'm still workin' on this one, based on a recipe from one of my antique cookbooks.

Dice up:

2 cups cooked chicken

1/2 cup mushrooms

1 small jar of roasted red peppers

Make a roux with flour and butter, add about a cup of chicken stock and half as much heavy cream, get that boiling and add the chicken, shrooms and peppers. Add a raw egg yolk, stir like crazy until the Queen gets thick. Salt, pepper, a little red pepper flakes; serve on toast and call it dinner!

Oh My Buns!

Food is love. Burgers are food. **So I gotta figure that burgers are love.** And you are going to love love LOVE my year's worth of tasty variations on this all-American classic! They might look simple but they took a lot of...well, not time but, you know, thought, and, like, creativity.

Breakfast Burger

You can eat this burger for B, L, D—or whip it up after a long night of heavy partying. It'll cure what ails you.

1 lb. ground beef
4 eggs
EVOO
Bacon bits
Home fries
Donuts

1. Fry up your burgers (if you don't know how to do this by now, just give it up).

2. Get that EVOO into a frying pan over high heat. Once it's almost smoking, drop your eggs in and fry them however you like (my fave is sunny side up).

3. Put the burger on top of the donut, top with an egg and sprinkle on some bacon bits. Top with another donut. (I guess if you wanted to you could slice one donut in half to make this more figure friendly...) Serve with the home fries, if you remember to make them.

A DONUT INSTEAD OF A BUN? *Fan-freakin'-tastic!* I like powdered sugar donuts for this, but you can use your fave, I guess.

Cranberry sauce inside the burger! How clever is that?

Thanksgiving Burger

1 lb. ground turkey
Stuffing mix
Chicken stock
Wholeberry cranberries
EVOO
Turkey gravy, heated up
Frozen mashed turnips, nuked until hot
Store-bought corn bread

I've explained the trick for getting the cranberry sauce inside this burger in *Rachell Ray's Freakin' Easy Holidays* (due on the Fourth of July, 2010).

Sicilian Burger

a/k/a Love on a Bun!

4 Italian sausage patties (hot or sweet)
1 can O-shaped spaghetti in sauce
4 slices hard salami
4 slices provolone
1 small can black olives, chopped
4 ciabatta buns

Fry up your sausages in some EVOO. Pile on "the love" and mangia!

Meat and Potatoes Burger

Do I even need to explain?

Your fave mashed potato recipe
1 pound ground beef
1 recipe "Oh My Gravy" (see Yumm-oh!)
4 hard or Kaiser rolls, sliced horizontally

Bun. Burger. Taters. A "well" for the gravy.

Veggie Burger

I would never actually eat this because...well, look at it! But even vegetarians have to eat.

1 veggie burger
Can of creamed corn
Can of lima beans
Can of baby peas

Fry up veggie burgers. Bun 'em. Top with veggies.

Yumbo Gumbo Burger Good luck with these!

1 pound ground beef

1 package andouille sausage;
run your knife through them to make a rough chop

1 jar pickled okra

1 can baby shrimp

Po' boy rolls

Combine meat and sausages, form patties and try to keep them in one piece in the pan (mixture will be uncooperative). Serve on po' boy rolls with pickled okra and baby shrimp on the side.

Mac n' Cheeseburger

Who says a "burger" has to include meat? Not me!

Boxed mac 'n cheese on a bun

Iceberg lettuce sliced into "confetti"

2 tomatoes, sliced

4 soft burger buns

Make the mac 'n cheese, pile it on the bun, garnish with lettuce and tomato.

Picnic Burger

What a burger! What a mess!

1 bag coleslaw

1 good scoop of mayo

Some celery salt

1 pound ground beef

1 can baked beans

2 or 3 dill pickles; run your knife through 'em

2 big handfuls of potato chips, crushed

4 hamburger buns

Make coleslaw. Make burgers. Top with beans, pickles, slaw, some chips and *voila!* (that's French for "You're good to go.")

Happy Burger: Three Ways

Sometimes even *I'm* amazed at what I get away with calling "recipes."

 **1** Ketchup

Ground beef

Ketchup smiley face

Bun

 2 Mustard

Ground beef

Yellow mustard smiley face

Bun

 3 Mayo

Ground beef

Mayo smiley face

Bun

My Big Fat Favorite Burger

Kobe beef, hand-crafted bacon and a fresh brioche bun—Yumm-oh!

Serves 1 and only 1. Go make your own.

1/2 lb. ground Kobe beef

2 large pieces of imported French butter, softened

4 slices nitrate-free, applewood-smoked artisan bacon

2 slices extra sharp cheddar cheese

1 Vidalia onion, sliced 1/4" thick

EVOO

1 sprig fresh thyme

French gray sea salt

Freshly ground black pepper

1 freshly baked brioche bun

1 slice vine-ripened tomato

2 lettuce leaves

Ketchup and mustard

These ingredients cost a little more, but I'm totally worth it!

Season onions with salt, pepper and thyme, sauté in EVOO until caramelized, about 25 minutes over low heat.

Knead butter into beef, season with salt and pepper, shape into one very large patty (it'll be about the size of a saucer). Brown on both sides, then finish cooking in a 375 degree oven until burger is medium rare. Top with cheese for the last five minutes to get just the right melt going.

Toast bun lightly, smear a little butter on it.

Assemble burger: start with the bun, put the burger on it, top with bacon, onions, tomato, and lettuce. Add condiments.

Find a secluded spot and get your chow on!

Deelishing with...

Some guy who has NO idea who I am!

How cool is this? You know how I sit down and dish with celebrities all the time and we take some photos and turn it into this monthly feature called "Deelishing with…"? Well, one of my producers, Gillian, was trying to get a famous star (I can't tell you who but she's got really big lips, and some people called her a homewrecker for a while, until she got involved with an international relief agency and started adopting babies from…gosh! everywhere!), but negotations just dragged on and on and, well, we ran out of time.

So Gills went out to have a little weepfest on the sidewalk because she knew I was going to be pissed off and she met this really cool guy who gave her a cigarette and rubbed her arm while she paced back and forth saying "I'm gonna get canned, she's gonna kill me, I'm gonnna get canned," etc.

And guess what? It turned out the guy HAD NO IDEA WHO I AM! Interesting, right?

That's what Gills thought. So she brings him up to the studio and sits him down and we had the *best* time DEElishing!

RR: Hey, guy, how is it possible you've never heard of me?
Guy: Um, I still don't know who you are, exactly.

RR: I'm Rachell! Rachell Ray! I make 30-minute meals, I travel around, I giggle. C'mon, I'm like totally famous even though I'm just a gal who's kind of a geek, y'know?
Guy: Ah, well…nice to meet you.

RR: I bet! So, guy. What's it like to be you, just minding your business out on the street, and all of a sudden you're sitting here with makeup on and a photographer buzzin' around while you talk to me?
Guy: Er, it's kind of weird. Actually, I was…

RR: It must be. So you've never seen any of my shows?
Guy: Not that I know of. Wait, are you that chick who cooks the Italian food?

RR: Yeah! That's me!
Guy: Wow! You're so much hotter on TV.

RR: What?
Guy: On TV you wear those low-cut blouses and you've got, y'know, a bigger chest and your dad is a movie guy, right?

RR: No, you're thinking of someone else. I'm the one who has a magazine.
Guy: You're Oprah?

RR: No, I'm not, Op…get this guy outta here! He doesn't even know who I am! Where's Gills? She is so getting fired. Gills! Gills! Don't you try to hide from me, you…
Guy: So, are we done here?

Find More Rachell On-line

at everyfreakingday.com

CROP CIRCLES

Join Rach when she visits Area 51 for tips at
everyfreakingday.com/aliens

INNER CIRCLES

Apply for membership in Rach's fan club at
everyfreakingday.com/clique

BUY CIRCLES

There are thousands of uses for our closeout on circles at
everyfreakingday.com/circles

New! Home Design On-line

Need some tips on making your home look its best? Check out my new online home design service—full of great ideas like slapping a coat of paint on outdated kitchen cabinets, clever uses for ordinary bed sheets, and so much more that it's gonna make your head spin!

everyfreakingday.com/home_design

Web Exclusive!

Clearance Corner

How cool are these?

MARSHMALLOW BURGER
(dozens in stock; make an offer)

CHAIR CANDLE HOLDER
(someone thought this was a good idea…)

PERKY PEPPER PLAQUE
(truly one of a kind)

Tricks of the Trade

Tactics for taking their minds off what's going on in the kitchen.

Entertaining isn't just about eating, it's also about lettin' the good times roll, as my granddaddy used to say. Sometimes you need a little somethin' somethin' to get your guests' minds off the food, if you know what I mean! Here are a couple of my tried and true tricks for turnin' up the volume on the fun-o-meter.

 Hey, you! Look at me!

The Carry*

Hey, kids! I'm *finally* revealing the secrets behind my signature move.

Step One: I grab a bunch of ingredients out of the fridge, pile it in my arms and walk over to the cupboard.

Step Two: I load up on even more stuff.

Step Three: I try to get to the counter without dropping anything —while keeping up the clever patter!

Patent Pending

Lube Job

When conversation starts to lag, I like to liven things up with my personal variation on a little game I found online called "The RR Drinking Game." It's easy, it's fun, and it's all about two of my favorite things—me and a nice cocktail.

tip

*For some reason, people ask me about hangover remedies all the time. I tell 'em my tried and true is a big ol' greasy diner breakfast and a giant ice-cold cola—**works like a charm!***

MY DRINKING GAME RULES

IF I:	COMPETITORS MUST:
Talk to the food	Take 2 sips
Give the food a nickname	Drain the glass
Say "totally"	Take 1 sip
Sing to the food	Drain the glass
Giggle	Take 1 sip
Call an ingredient "a little thing that makes 'em go 'what the hell?'"	Drain 2 glasses
Mention that any food is "nutty"	Take 2 sips
Say "eyeball it"	Take 2 sips
Say "hello" to the food	Take 1 sip
"Invent" a word	Drain the glass
Put an ingredient "down over the top of" a dish	Take 1 sip
Call guests "kids"	Drain the bottle

The Daily Grind

When it comes to coffee, I like super-caffeinated and plenty of it! But I'm no barista—in fact, I don't even know how to make instant. Which is why I don't understand why the staff here at *Every Freaking! Day* thought testing a bunch of coffee paraphernalia was such a good idea. Hello? I don't bake and I don't brew. What next, biscotti recipes?

French press: Precise measurements, careful timing—this thing is as complicated as a Swiss timepiece!

Everything in this magazine is on sale at **everyfreakingday.com!** Talk about convenient! How simple is that?

Coffee grinder
How do you know when to stop?

Automatic single-cup, pod system coffee maker:
One little cup at a time? Are you freaking kidding me?

Coffee To Go Go Go:
Listen, I didn't land a major promo deal for a certain coffee purveyor for nothin'. I run on this stuff!

We Are Fam-i-ly

I'm a big advocate of spur of the moment get-togethers, but a family reunion is "a whole other animal," as my granddaddy used to say. This kind of party takes oodles of planning. The first step is always deciding where to have your bash. Because my families don't get together too often, I wanted to make sure the venue was just as special as this event.

To: editor@RRWorldwide
From: RR@RRWorldwide
Re: Family Reunion location

Got your email re: having this at my new house and just have to say: ARE YOU OUT OF YOUR FREAKING MIND? There is NO WAY that's happening. First of all, I barely know half these people. Second, I don't want half my stuff showing up on eBay. Third of all, NO FREAKING WAY!

Ha ha! These are great. Just make sure that we replace them with the "real" copy before this goes to the printer
...RR!

Countdown to Disaster

Kidding! Totally kidding! I love my families...

Getting the whole family to the same location on the same day takes as much planning as a full-scale invasion. So Mammaretto* and I started prepping months in advance.

To: Mamma@RRWorldwide
From: RR@RRWorldwide
Subject: Family Reunion

Ma! Whether you like it or not, this thing is happening. It's on the editorial calendar, so get on board.

To : RR@RRWorldwide
From: Mamma@RRWorldwide
Subject: Re: Family Reunion

Just don't invite your father....

*"Mammaretto" is just one of my mom's many nicknames. This one was inspired by a certain incident involving the famous amaretto liqueur of Italy...Oh, Mamma! It took days for her to recover from that one!

Hey, Kids — It's Family Reunion Time!
When: First Saturday in October
Time: 1 p.m. to whenever!
Where: The Family Homestead
RSVP via email to CousinRach@RR.org

Hope to see all y'all!

Hey, Kids
It's Family Reunion Time!

When: First Saturday in October
Time: Noon to whenever!
Where: The Family Homestead

RSVP via email to
CousinRach@RR.org

Speranza vederli tutti!

I wanted to make sure both sides of the fam felt special, so I included a little Italian on some invites and some down-home "lingo" on the others.

Separate warring clans at the dinner table according to ethnicity, class, taste, and quality of food and place settings.

My uncle, Regus Patoff Lesboeuf. He and my Tante Baby were named after their mama's favorite food—canned Baby LeSueur Peas; his name is a variation on the phrase "Registered with U.S. Patent Office." ("Reg. U.S. Pat. Off." Get it?)

This is Big Vito, my mom's oldest brother and patriarch of the Scuderia clan. We were really lucky he could make it, because he had "a potential conflict of interest." Look at how excited he is!

Hey! You know what's really fun? Forcing a reunion on family members who hate each other's freaking guts! Ha! Ha! Ha!

I love this picture because these two have only been able to maintain their truce by keeping a distance of 6 states between them, but they came together for me!

There's an old Italian saying:

There's nothing wrong with asking "the fam" to contribute a little something to cover the cost of a big family party. In fact, I've found that people really want to show their generosity in situations like this. And if they don't…well, there's an old Italian saying that goes like this: "O mangiar questa minestra o saltar questa finestra." That means, "Either eat this soup or jump out this window," or as I like to say, "Hey, kids, take it or leave it."

```
WELCOME TO OUR QUESTS

Sisters of the Easter Star lunchion        12:00-2:30

Opus Dei monthly meeting                   2:45-5:00

Scuderia-Ray Ramily Renunion*              5:15-6:15

National Association of Podiatrists
Annual Dinner Dance                        7:00-midnight


* $20.00 cover
```

My little cousins Bubba and Vito meet for the first time.

Wow! What are the odds of this happening?

I value my privacy, so I never allow my homes to be photographed (unless I'm just renting). I had to find a spot that was fun and funky. Lucky for me, I found this place that's totally neutral territory PLUS the rent is CHEAP! Double bonus!

I decided to send everyone home with a little memento of the big event.

The best advice I have for a big event like this is KISS—Keep It Simple, Sistah!

I ordered everything from the tablecloths up to all the food, from my warehouse deli "catering service."

Oh my gravy! Can you say "kissin' cousins?"

Sometimes a little special magic happens between two people, and the fact that they might be related just doesn't matter. That's Baby Doucette DuRay ("Baby" after her mother, "Doucette" because she's so darned sweet) and "Ferrari" Scuderia, whose nickname is totally right on. No one saw this one coming, but I guess it's true: There *is* a lid for every pot! Maybe we'll be hearing church bells—the happy kind—at our next family reunion.

I was going to show you the menu my mom and I came up with that had great family dishes like Auntie Griselda's Austrian Dreams, Fake-'Em-Out Carbonera, and the classic Vendetta Cake (because revenge is a dish best eaten cold). But we ran out of space, so, I decided to gather all those recipes—and more—in my new cookbook: *Rachell Ray's Family Reunion*, comin' at ya in plenty of time for *your* next get-together.

You know, when I first thought about throwing this bash, I was a little worried. But now the whole family is here and the food is on the table—does it get any better than this? Sure it does—somebody open the wine!

Uncle Regus sure does love my "secret recipe" fried chicken!

You can never tell what's gonna set off someone in my famiglia...

Family is all about sharing.
Here the whole gang is playing "Pass the bread, please!" Little Bubba's so happy he's dancing a Cajun jig!

Y'know, I never get to eat at parties because I'm too busy dancing and talking and making sure everyone's glass is full. So my favorite part of every party is after everyone's gone, when I get to sit down, think about how much fun we had, and actually chow down.

The overnight bestseller from one of the fastest cookbook authors of our time!

"A real page-turner—for the author, NOT THE READER."

– The Picayunne Times

"Scary-fast!" – Richard Petty

"Chock full of down-home dishes and real-time advice for anyone who has reason to believe Rach's family might drop by for supper someday."

– Paula Deane, author
The Lard's Prayer: Cookin' in Pork Fat Heaven!

"THE must-have gift of the year!"
– R. Ray

RACHELL RAY'S
FAMILY REUNION
GREAT MEALS FOR RELATIVES

A 30-SECOND MEAL COOKBOOK

web

Order several today at
everyfreakingday.com

A Day in the Diet of a Mystery Taster

Guess who! Ya know how on my show a famous person stops by to taste what I'm cooking and I have to figure out who they are? Now it's your turn. Here's a hint: He used to be "the leader of the free world."

BREAKFAST

This isn't how I want to start my days, but a few years ago I had quadruple by-pass surgery. Talk about a wake up call! That's when I realized that I had to put the brakes on eating the foods I've loved since childhood—like sausage gravy on a biscuit (or two). So most mornings I have a cup of black coffee and something boring like this. Then me and "the boys" (that's what I call my Secret Service detail) hit the pavement for our daily run.

MIDNIGHT SNACK

I'm not proud of this. But if there's one thing I've learned it's that it's better to come clean about one's transgressions immediately, so here are the facts: It was late. I was hungry. The cupboard was bare. I mobilized "the boys" and we hit the mini-mart—hard. I'm gonna miss that place when we move back to D.C. in January.

LUNCH

It's soup. Vegetable soup. Healthy. Ya-freakin'-hoo.

DINNER

On the rare nights that I'm actually home for dinner, there's nothing like a bowl of whole wheat pasta primavera. Yep. Nothin' like it.

tip

Now that's what I call moderation! You don't have to deny yourself, just indulge in smaller portions of your favorite pig-out foods.

It's 'Wich-Craft

Here's a baker's half-dozen of my fave sammies!

Anyone can slap meat and stuff between two slices of bread and call it a sandwich. But only I make *sammies*, which is one of the reasons they pay me the big bucks. And I have to admit that I'm especially proud of this batch because I think I've stretched the whole sammie genre, if I do say so myself.

tip

Don't be afraid to take a little help from the store and use prepackaged/prepared foods.

Editor's Note:
We apologize for the fact that there are only 5 sandwiches. Apparently Rachell was a little confused about what constitutes a "baker's dozen."

CREAM OF CHICKEN SOUP

MOZZA-RELLA

BREAD

GABBA-GOOL

SWISS

EVOO

HEAD CHEESE

BUTTER

DEVILED HAM

JALAPEÑO

SAUER-KRAUT

BOLOGNA

LETTUCE

ALL ON BOARD FOR SAMMIES!
A tasty meal is just seconds away!

I call this sammi "Mister" because he's one big super-stuffed fella, if you know what I mean. My inspiration was the famous Croque Monsieur—that's French for "Mr. Sammi"—but I add some Italian twists in honor of my Sicilian heritage.

Mr. Sammi

4 knuckles of butter, softened (that's about 4 tablespoons)

1 can cream of chicken soup

3/4 lb. gabbagool (capacolla ham)

2 cups shredded mozzarella (one of those sacks is just the right size—go fat-free for a figure-friendly version)

EVOO (that's extra virgin olive oil)

8 slices of semolina bread

....

Lay your bread out on a cutting board. Spread 2 knuckles of butter on the outside of the bread. On the unbuttered side, spread a thick layer of your soup and top with the gabbagool. Add a layer of mozz. Now, slap those suckers together to make 4 sammies.

In a large skillet, melt the rest of the butter with the EVOO—about 3 passes around the pan. Lay those sammies in that vat and fry away, about 3 minutes on each side.

BLD (Bologna, Lettuce, Deviled Ham)

My mom used to whip up these open-faced sammies when she ran a high-end smorgasbord restaurant. You can *totally* entertain with these!

....

4 slices of soft white sandwich bread

One package pre-sliced bologna

One bag shredded iceberg lettuce

One can deviled ham

EVOO (extra virgin olive oil)

....

Smear the bread with the deviled ham. Top with slices of bologna and a shower of lettuce. Drizzle with EVOO, serve and enjoy!

Don't know who came up with this idea, but this recipe totally doesn't work. Why would we just slap a slice of ham on a burger bun?

RR

(a/k/a The Boss Lady)

A Real Hamburger

Ever wonder why a patty of ground beef is called a hamburger? Me, too! Makes no sense at all, right? This sammi totally fixes that mistake... No need to thank me, I'm here to serve.

....

1 canned ham

1 large onion

1/2 head of garlic

Mayo (pull out your industrial-size jar, you're going to need it)

Sweet pickle relish

EVOO (extra virgin olive oil)

Ketchup

Mustard

....

1. Open the can, scrape off that weird gelatin stuff (you can save it for your next Head Case Sammi), run a knife through the ham to break it down into chunks. Drop them in your food processor. Now do a rough chop on the onion and garlic, drop 'em in the processor and slap the top on. Give it a coupla turns until the whole mess looks like ground meat. Spoon in some mayo and relish, open up the lid and see if it will stick together. If it doesn't, add more mayo.

2. Heat up a large skillet, pour in some EVOO (a couple of turns around the pan). Form the ham mixture into patties, slap 'em in the pan and fry until golden brown on both sides. Serve on the buns, top with ketchup and mustard. Yumm-Oh!

Head Case Sammi

I know, I know—you hear the words "head cheese" and just think "eeeewwww!" Well, so did I until one late night when all I wanted was something with a certain gelatinous quality, something "gelatifabulous!" Then it hit me: Head cheese. I made a beeline to the all-night deli and this was the result.

....

Day-old rye bread

1/4 lb. head cheese

1 small can sauerkraut, drained

Coupla slices o' swiss

Yellow mustard

....

Stack two slices of head cheese on a slice of bread. Top with sauerkraut and cheese. Squirt on a flood of mustard. Slap another piece of bread on the whole shebang, crack open a nice cold brewski, and have at it.

Grown-Up PBJ&J

Pickled jalapeños add a little kick to the lunchbox classic. Now that's what I'm talkin' about! How do I come up with this stuff?

If These Hands Could Talk

Oh, wait, they *do* talk!

I'm Italian so I talk with my hands, which must be sort of like speaking a foreign language because people ask me what all the gestures are about all the time. To clear up the mystery, we decided to provide you with a handy guide to my hands. (Get it? Get it? "A *handy* guide…" Eh, what am I gonna do with you people? Which is exactly what my first gesture means!)

"This is a real multitasker of a hand signal, because I use it a lot. So it could mean anything from, 'I really groove on this' to 'How cool is that?' to 'Another endorsement deal? Yes!'"

"So you can't make the food as fast as I do on the show, whaddaya want from me? What are you, a baby? Should I call a 'whaaaa-mbulence' for you?"

"Steal second!" or "Fuggetaboudit!" (which I always say like I'm in a *Godfather* movie or *Goodfellas*).

"I swear, if you think you don't like [fill in the blank with some kind of food], you couldn't be more wrong."

"Hey! Ask me again about when I lived in Denmark, you chooch, and I'll…."

"You know, it's so very hard to be humble when you're this stinkin' adorable."

"Sometimes it just hits me that I get paid over $10 million a year! Yay for me!"

Swell Swill

and Food to Match!

One of the biggest challenges facing vino lovers is finding a bottle that won't put a strain on the old pocketbook. We looked high and low for wines that deliver great drinkability and even greater value and, by golly, we found some! Not in the same bottles, but, hey, whaddya want?

Bottom of the Barrel Berry Wine, $5.99

We unearthed this baby from the absolute bottom shelf of a package store in the middle of nowhere. What a find! This "wine" was full of surprises—as light-bodied as water, as fruity as Kool-Aid, and non-existent tannins.

Pair it with

Manicotti-Angel Hair Bundles with Red Clam Sauce

Look up "hearty" in the dictionary and you'll find a photo of this rib-sticking powerhouse! Combine two kinds of pasta, a can of Manhattan clam chowder, pop it in the oven for an hour. Now that's what I call carbo-loading!

Find these recipes—and more —in "30-Second Meals," page 49.

everyfreakingday.com

Opus One and A Half, $3.82

Full-bodied, really dark Italian-style red, and best of all you can keep it on ice so it will last for years! Though it lacks finesse, this wine more than makes up for that by being completely without complexity.

Pair it with

Turkey Spam Stir Fry

Opus One and A Half brings just the right touch to the table for this one-dish meal. You can totally entertain with my figure-friendly Turkey Spam Stir Fry the next time your friends drop by without an invite! That'll teach 'em.

Duck, Duck, Goose Ya!, $5.97

A sweet combination of red and white wines blended with a soft Concord-grape base, this is a wine that is perfect for an Every Freaking Day celebration.

Dried Beef Carpaccio

Pair it with

Carpaccio is usually made with super-thin slices of beef tenderloin, but I think this version is even better, 'cause it's jam-packed with salt and if there's one thing I can't get enough of, it's salt! It's elegant, it's easy and making the carpaccio from jarred dried beef makes it super pocket-book friendly.

Why Not White?, $4

A cross between an un-oaked chardonnay and a muscadet, Why Not White? is light on the tongue and goes down as easy as soda pop.

Pair it with

Chicken Nuggets Salad

There are two things I really love—chicken nuggets, French fries and a good white wine. Wait, that's three things I really love. Plus my dog. Oh, and my sweetie. And my mom, how did I forget her? So, let's see, that's six things I really love. This dish satisfies on all counts—it's got the nuggets and the fries, I can share it with the people I love, and I always serve it with plenty of wine. What could be better?

Dining on the Downlow

A girl's gotta eat, but it doesn't have to break the bank.

When I was growing up, my family owned a bunch of restaurants. After things went bad (a *looooong* story), my mom managed about 150 restaurants that this guy owned. Needless to say, we spent a lot of time checking out the competition and one of our favorite things to do as a family was to see how little we could spend while still enjoying as many courses as was humanly possible.

The dining ethic instilled by my mama has always served me well. In fact, my skill at finding delectable meals that don't break the bank has totally paid off—my success at dining on the cheap was the inspiration for two of my TV shows: *$29.99 A DAY* and *TOOTHSOME TOURS*.

This issue, I'm sharing how you can dine on the cheap in style at some of the most famous restaurants in the Big Apple (that's Manhattan, NYC, NY).

> **Hey, you!** While you're waiting for your table in a restaurant, hang out near the bar's garnish tray and snack on the olives, maraschino cherries and orange slices—that way you won't waste your hard-earned moola on appetizers!

Big Bang

LA COAT BRUSQUE has a big rep and big prices to match—twenty bucks for a starter of escargot, three times that for a half of a roasted chicken. Yikes! Because I really groove on value, I decided to prorate the price of my meal. I ate smaller portions of each dish and adjusted my bill accordingly. This is a really simple technique that anyone can use to make dining out more budget friendly.

Big Glamour

Because I've been hearing about **"THE 20 CLUB"** since I was a kid, I expected it to be "classy." What a pleasant surprise to find that I could get a big bucket 'o burgers for just $9.99! I never did see any celebrities or the famous collection of lawn jockeys, though. The moral of that story is to always choose your dining spot wisely.

I went back later and tipped my server. I swear, I did.

Big Surprise

When I visited it, the famous Upper East Side eatery **CAFÉ DES DILETTANTES** was full of actor/waiters, wannabe food writers and chefs who were "between kitchens" (which is code for unemployed). Everything I tasted was dee-lish, especially the appetizers and the specialty cocktails, but the best part was that the entire meal ended up being on the house after someone on the staff recognized me!

Big Guns

As soon as I walked into **FRANKIE FOUR-FINGER'S CHOP & DROP BUTCHER SHOP** on 11th Ave, I knew I was outta my league and in for a big tab. So I made the best of it by ordering the house special tasting menu along with a couple of bottles of really good wines from Tuscany. When the check came, I whipped out the corporate AmEx and added a tip that could be called "very nice." Can you say "expense account"?

Floaters!

Sometimes it's nice to come home to something that's all ready to eat, you know? Even though most of the time my life is a blur of hosting celebrities on my talk show (you've seen it, right?), taping my cooking shows and writing my cookbooks, every once in a while even I get cravings for dishes that take some pre-planning. That's when I turn to these classic floaters.

RR Time Saver:
To cut down on clean-up, forget about utensils and use your hands. After all, they're the best tools you've got, right?

"Back in the Day" Party Mixup

One of my favorite things when I was a kid was when we had parties, because my dad always made his famous party mix, which I washed down with plenty of fruit-flavored drink mix. My Party Mixup combines those two great tastes in one gleaming dish.

1 recipe party mix (it's on the box)
1 box mixed fruit flavored gelatin

Make the mix, pour it into a gelatin mold, add the prepared gelatin. Put it in the chill-box until it sets. Slice and serve!

Swamp Thang Fruit Salad

It looks kinda like something out of an old horror movie, right? That's why I call it Swamp Thang.

1 can fruit salad
1 package mini marshmallows
1 box orange flavored gelatin

Mix it. Mold it. Chill it.

Everybody Into the Pool!

You know what they say. "Gravity sucks." So this one didn't work out exactly the way I planned it. But when life sends you sinkers instead of floaters, I say "toss 'em a lifesaver!" Ah, I kill myself with these jokes!

1 dozen chocolate covered peanut and nougat "fun-size" candies
1 box blue gelatin

Put the candies in a shallow dish. Pour the prepared gelatin down over the top. Don't be alarmed when the color leaches out of the chocolate; it'll taste just fine.

Brats and Beer Floaters

Some things just go together. I used a really pale ale for this combo.

1 package bratwurst
A six pack of the most affordable beer you can find.

Place 1 brat in each stein, top with the brewski.

Big Deal!

Rach's design buddy, Buddy, gives a small kitchen a sparkling makeover!

My home makeover maven Buddy gave homeowners Judy and Punch a whole kitchen makeover in just a few hours! How awesome is that?!

Cheap Fix:
Buy some cleaning supplies (they cost about $10) and move a rug in from another room.

 HOUR ONE
Load and run dishwasher, hand wash and dry pots and pans.

 HOUR TWO
Put stuff away where it belongs; clean counters, fronts of appliances and cupboards.

HOUR THREE
Wash floor. When dry, lay down new kitchen rug.

Q&A with Rachell Ray

(Hey, that rhymes! How cool is that?)

Q: Rach, I keep having a dream that you and I are hanging out, traveling to cool places, under-tipping and mooching free stuff. Do you ever have one of those kind of dreams?

RR: About you? Nope. And don't call me "Rach."

Q: How come your voice sounds like you're a washed out old bar hag who's just finished smoking a pack of cigarettes with no filters?

RR: Just lucky I guess. A lot of the women in my family sound like this.

Q: I'm confused. You used to talk about being a "Southern girl," about having a "Cajun granddaddy who cooked his roux all day," but now you say you're Sicilian through and through. What happened?

RR: Well a lot of people don't understand that, bottom line, the Cajuns and Southerners are Sicilians. I don't quite get it myself, so I've asked Dr. Clarence Schuquester, an expert on migrational anthropology, to explain. Take it away, Doc!

Hello! I'm listenin'!

Q: I really love your magazine! Does it take you a long time to come up with all those great ideas?

RR: I love it, too!

Q: Now that you're famous, isn't it hard to do normal stuff, like going to the grocery store and picking up tampons and stuff like that?

RR: Oh no. I've got people for that.

Q: The other night I decided to try one of your "30-minute meals" and, long story short, it took a helluva lot longer—more like 90 minutes. What gives?

RR: Y'know, when I get home and open up that first bottle of vino, it can take me up to an hour to make dinner and that's okay. The bottom line is, you need the right tools—like my knives, my cookware, my prep cooks...

> There is a common misconception that all Cajun people were part of the vast diaspora of French Acadians in the late-18th century. While it is true that some of these Acadians migrated to Louisiana and became so-called "Cajuns," they did so by intermarriage with an already extant group—the original Cajuns—who had arrived directly from Sicily some 500 years earlier. Miss Rachell Ray is a direct descendant of a clan of original Cajuns. In fact, I'm using her uniquely pure DNA to definitively prove my claims about the original Cajuns that those short-sighted idiots who refer to me as a renegade refuse to consider on the grounds that I've been thus far unsuccessful in adequately explaining this mysterious migration. "Unfounded pie in the sky pseudo-anthropology," my ass! How else to explain the strange propensity for using garlic in all foods? Who but the Sicilians used that much garlic!? Those smug bastards! Historical data? It proves nothing, nothing! When I get all my research in place, I'm gonna win the goddamned Nobel Prize! Obviously they used space ships!
> —Dr. Schuquester

RR: So, see, it really *does* all go back to Sicily.

No Time? No Sweat!

Yikes! When you're as busy as me—starring on multiple TV shows and commercials, showing up on all the morning, afternoon and evening talk shows, writing an entire magazine plus all those cookbooks all by myself AND those frequent coffee breaks—sometimes I can't even find thirty minutes to put together a meal. But a girl's gotta put something on the table, right? This is a meal that you can feed to family and friends without even breakin' a sweat.

Rachell's Save the Airfare "Sardine-ia" Pasta

I've combined the classic flavors of an ancient Sardinian dish in a whole new way.

....

Bag o' salad for roughage
Can o' pasta for pasta
Pitted prunes for a little sweet surprise
Sardines packed in oil, because they're sardines

....

Mix all this stuff together in a pretty serving bowl and put it on the table.

Rachell's Own Stylist Reveals All

Take one look at me, and you can tell I don't know the first thing about fashion. In fact, if I could I'd spend my life in sweats and a baseball cap. At the same time, a girl in my position has gotta rock "a look." It's a dilemma, for sure. That's why I'm completely dependent on Jane Haddison Coyote, my super-stylist. She picks out all my outfits—including my underwear! How weird is that? Anywho, this month Jane's dishing up her tips for dressing to look your best.

We start every day with a blank slate.

You see what I'm working with here...

"Sweats and a base-ball cap. Oy."

The sad truth is that all the money in the world can't buy a sense of style or good taste. It can, however, buy a stylist who will at least try to save you from true fashion disaster. I do what I can. Because Rachell sometimes—how do I put this?—burns the candle at both ends and doesn't always start the day looking as fresh and perky as we need her to be.

Thank God for cosmetics and good lighting!

Hey, I work hard, I play hard— that's what I call "goin' for the gusto," kids!

Rachell loves what she calls "the vintage look." I'd be completely and utterly lost without thrift stores.

tip

When in doubt, go with neutrals. Because they go with everything.

Because Rachell travels so much, she needs a wardrobe that can go anywhere—from sightseeing to a "lunch date" to dinner in an elegant restaurant. The obvious choice is jeans. Considering she's giving these places free publicity, who's going to complain?

Rachell's Rules

1. **Flaunt it, baby!** What's the point of downplaying your assets? If you have an itty-bitty waist like I do, play it up!

2. **Disguise and conquer.** Everybody has a "challenging body part," even me! Just remember that the right clothes can hide a multitude of sins.

3. **Remember**—comfort is key.

4. **Hire a stylist!** I got nothing else…

Jane's Rules for Rachell

5. **Choose fabrics that give and forgive.** One word—Lycra.®

6. **Size is a state of mind.** No matter what she weighs, Rachell swears she's a size 6, so I cut out all those little size labels in her wardrobe.

7. **Always let the star make the final decision.** If she wants to wear snap-crotch bodysuits from the 70s or some other tacky thing, let her.

Ta-da!
The finished product.

Hit the Road, Jack!

I don't know who this guy Jack is, but if he's footing the bill for a nice vacation, I am *sooooo* there! When I was told that this month's travel piece was going to include Venice, Rome, and Naples, I dug out my passport, put on my favorite travel outfit and…hit the road! (It seemed a little odd to me at first that no one was speaking Italian but, hey, I guess that's what happens when the tourist dollar rules.)

Where I Went – Day 1

Venice

> **When I went to Venice, I discovered that my dream had become—incredibly but quite simply—my address.**
> —*Marcel Proust*

What does that mean?

Venice is world famous for its canals. And its gondolas. And its carnival, when everyone in town wears a mask. Because I like to fit in wherever I go, when I was packing, I made sure I had some galoshes, a life jacket and a really cool mask that I found—"The Joker" from Batman!

Our first stop was for breakfast. We found a great coffee place where I had a big cup o' joe (black, no sugar) and a tasty breakfast pastry called a "doughnut." Dee-lish! Then it was time for some sightseeing. One great surprise was that there were a lot of palm trees!

2401 – ONE OF THE CANAL BRIDGES, VENICE, CALIFORNIA.

That's me in Venice, one of the most romantic cities in the entire world.

tip

Ask the locals. If they don't know, who will?

Hey You! The best way to get a deal anywhere—dinner and drinks on the house, great hotel rates, you name it!—is to always travel with a film crew. If you don't have one handy, make your sweetie or other travel companion follow you around with a video-cam. I'm telling ya, this totally works!

Where I Went – Day 2

Naples

BAY OF NAPLES INN, NAPLES, MAINE.

> In Napoli where love is King, When boy meets girl, here's what they say: When the moon hits your eye like a big-a pizza pie, that's amore…
> — *Harry Warren and Jack Brooks*

By the time we hit Naples, I was really looking forward to a pizza—which was invented right there sometime back in the day. Weird thing was, there was only one pizza place in the whole town and to tell you the truth, if this is the birthplace of pizza, it's a damn good thing that people migrated, if you catch my drift.

And, you know, it wasn't as warm as I expected it to be.

Architecture, schmarcitecture— where's the freakin' pizza?

Rome wasn't built in a day, but after about an hour I was ready for Splitsville.

Where I Went – Day 3

Rome

> Rome was a poem pressed into service as a city.
> — *Anatole Broyard*

One of my favorite cities of all time! Rome rocks! I could hardly wait to dig in to some of my favoritest Roman delicacies, like spaghetti carbonara (the Roman version of bacon and eggs), gelato (the Roman version of ice cream), and some excellent vino (the Roman version of wine).

But when we arrived, something seemed…off, somehow. No Coliseum, no Vatican, no Trevi Fountain. Just this post office. In fact, the landscape looked oddly familiar to me. In fact, if I didn't know any better, I'd have thought I was in upstate NY, near the Adirondacks, where I live in my little cabin.

Post Office, Rome, N. Y.

Messes and Total Disasters

My Readers *Rock!*

Sometimes the best ideas I get come from readers. Unfortunately, when I try to pass them off as my own, these people get all bent outta shape and the lawyers get involved and things get ugly. So we decided to dedicate a page to the great ideas—and funny stories about Total Disasters—my fans have so generously chosen to share!

Help me!

Margaritas have always been a fave with my crowd, but now that we're getting a little older and metabolisms are slowing down, none of us can afford all those calories. I came up with this figure-friendly "fakeout" that tastes exactly like the real thing, except for the weird aftertaste. Now every weekend party features Marji's Mess-a Fiesta Marjiaritas.

—MARJORIE P., *Levittown, NY*

- -

1 container artificially-sweetened, artificially-flavored and artificially-colored lemonade powder

4 shots tequila

3/4 blender ice

1 liter bottle of diet grapefruit soda

- -

Pour the first 3 ingredients into a blender, process on liquefy for about a minute, transfer to a large pitcher. Fill individual glasses halfway, top with grapefruit soda and enjoy!

- -

Rach's Take: Artificial sweetener is gross! Because I eat the right foods, I can indulge in straight shots of tequila—much more healthful and you get a buzz faster, too.

Early in our marriage, I decided to surprise my then-husband, Hansel, with a "special treat" involving plastic wrap and a big pre-made bow. Unfortunately, what should have been a little naughty fun turned into a Total Disaster when his mother, Nina, showed up to surprise us both with his favorite dinner—her home-made lasagna. Things went from bad to worse when she completely misunderstood my intentions and decided to "go natural" herself. The good news is we made a true love connection. Now my ex is my son-in-law and Nina's lasagne is my favorite dinner, too. Nina and I laugh about it now, but Hansel remains somewhat sensitive about the whole thing.

— GRETEL B-K-B., *Northhampton, MA*

- -

Rach's Take: What, no recipe? Where's the freakin' lasagna recipe?

One of my favorite things is watching your daily talk show, and my favorite thing ever was your contest for people who claimed they could cook. Rach, watching you revel in the losers' misery on elimination days was prime entertainment! **A TOTAL DISASTER**, indeed! Well done.

- -

Rach's Take: I totally got into giving those trained professional chefs the boot.

web

If you missed even a moment of the **CONTEST FOR PEOPLE WHO CLAIM THEY CAN COOK,** don't you worry! DVDs of the complete season are available at **everyfreakingday.com**

Bedtime Story

I gotta tell ya, on those rare days when I don't have to work non-stop, there's nothing I love more than spending a day in bed. You've got your jammies, your sweetie, your pup; what could be better?

Snacks, that's what! There's something about lounging around that brings out the Snackin' Monster in me.

On my last rare day off, I remembered that I'd invited some of my neighbors over for a "pay-back" meal. Talk about a buzz kill. Then I realized, "Hey, Rach, you can totally entertain in bed! Just whip up a couple of your oh-so-fast recipes, throw a drop cloth over the comforters and invite everyone to pile on."

So I did. And now you can, too, because I'm big on sharing my great ideas with all my fans. Here's a sneak peak of the first pages of *Rachell Ray's EZ Entertaining for Lay-Z-Daze—* coming to your favorite bookstore or website any time now.

Snackies for Lay-Z-Daze!

Entertaining in the bedroom is simple, cheap and easy. My "bed party go-tos" more than fit the bill, and did I mention that I have another new cookbook filled with even more recipes? Pick up a copy today and you'll be ready to welcome a crowd in your boudoir (that's French for bedroom) tonight.

It's a Wrap!

When you're eating in bed, finger foods are an absolute must. But you also need something that will stick to your ribs. That's why I invented this new take on a breakfast wrap that incorporates the flavors of a full Sunday brunch.

1 package whole wheat wraps
1 package pre-cooked bacon
Maple syrup

Wrap the wrap around the bacon. Pour some maple syrup in a little bowl and dip away!

Aunt Griselda's Austrian Dreams

My great-aunt Griselda (my dad's mom's sister) was engaged for a while to an Austrian count, but he died in a tragic accident. She invented this dish in honor of her lost love.

1 can Vienna sausages
1 package frozen Brussels sprouts
1 jar cheese dip

For each Dream, place 2 sprouts and 1 sausage on a skewer. When you're ready to serve, heat up the cheese dip and place in an attractive bowl.

A little fruit is a great way to round out your meal. Bananas are a no-brainer: just drop a bunch down over the sheets and let everybody grab one.

Bananas

Hell-oh, Mr. Nanner! Do you know how many bananas are consumed in the U.S. of A. every year? Neither do I, but it's probably a LOT!

....

1 bunch bananas

....

Bananas have great appeal, but you'll want to remove that. A peel/appeal. Is a joke funny if you have to explain it? I keep my garbage bowl nearby to make it EZ to discard the peels.

Karaoke, anyone?

One fun idea is to make everybody serenade the bananas: I love that old Tin Pan Alley tune, **"YES, WE HAVE NO BANANAS!"** because I'm all about the irony. But people can really get their groove on with **"THE BANANA BOAT SONG."**

I keep nuts, fruit leather and spiced beef snack sticks on hand for quick energy.

Greek Yogurt with Honey

Hell-oh, Mr. Acidopholus and Miss Honey!

....

1 container Greek yogurt
1 squirt bottle honey

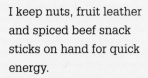

I like to keep my grillin' machine right near the bed for those sudden cravings for a nice Italian sausich.

tip

Wear jammies with an elastic waistband, so you can really enjoy this "all you can eat" buffet.

It's EZ to make even the simplest dish miraculous.

Ya Gotta Feed 'Em Something

Some people have children and other people (like me and the sweetie) have four-legged "kids." Either way, you gotta love 'em and ya gotta feed 'em. I asked my good friend and famous chef, Mario Catali, to come on over and help me cook up a feast for his kids and mine. Here's what we came up with.

Mario's Dishes

You can find all of Mario's recipes on **everyfreakingday.com**, if you want. But believe you me, they are waaaaaay too much work for something you're going to feed a kid. Or a dog. So I decided to skip 'em and go straight to the good, simple stuff.

Crunch and Munch

My "kid" Itsadog loves to share a meal with her favorite rugrats. When she's having a play date, I often serve up this snackie that lets them get up close and personal with one another.

Dry dog food
"O" shaped oat cereal
Milk

Pour the dog food into one small compartment of a "kiddie" plate.

Pour cereal into the other smaller compartment.

Pour milk into the biggest compartment.

Set it down and step out of the way.

Rach's Two-fer Tuna

When you've got a passel of hungry little-bitties underfoot, you need to make something quick and easy! This dish is perfect for kids of the two- and four-legged varieties.

1 can tuna

2 handfuls breadcrumbs or rice or leftover pasta

Mayo

Hot sauce

EVOO (that's Extra Virgin Olive Oil)

Water

Snack crackers (I use the kind that have a picture of me on the box)

Find a can opener, open the can.

In a food processor, mix all the ingredients (except for the crackers) into a paste.

Spread the paste on crackers.

Serve.

Sit back and wait for the howls of joy!

I call mayo Yuko but the kids seem to like it AND it gives 'em a good, shiny coat.

TUNA QUIZ

Who invented tuna salad?

A. the Phoenicians

B. an Albanian

C. somebody from New Jersey.

ANSWER:
D. None of the above. It just comes that way.

Helloooo, Mr. Grape! (kids love to talk to their food)

These tiny bundles of fiber give kids of all kinds a little "get up and go" (wink, nudge—you know what I'm talking about).

If your kids think they don't like onions and garlic, they're wrong.

Everybody knows that onions are a big "no no" for dogs—at least they know it now, thanks to me. And kids, apparently, are born with some weird onion phobia that makes them pout and cry and do all sorts of stuff that practically guarantees a spot on Santa's "bad little girls and boys" list. I don't get it—I loved all of the veggies when I was a kid—but I guess that's because Grampy Emilio grew everything in his organic garden so everything, including onions, was as sweet as candy.

So here's what I do when I'm cooking for kids and they claim to hate onions and garlic: I tell them they're candy. **Works every freaking time.**

Recipes I Couldn't Fit Anywhere Else

Manicotti-Angel Hair Bundles with Red Clam Sauce

(PAIR IT WITH BOTTOM OF THE BARREL BERRY WINE)

Should serve 6, if you can convince anyone to actually eat this mess.

6 manicotti shells

1/2 pound angel hair pasta

1 19-ounce can Manhattan clam chowder
(I call it "chowdah" because I'm a Cape Cahd gahl)

EVOO to coat the pan, plus some more

Parmigiano Reggiano

Salt and Pepper

Preheat your oven to 350 degrees. Coat an 8"x 8" baking dish with olive oil (a couple of turns around the dish, about 1/4 cup), set aside.

Get that angel hair pasta down into the manicotti shells. Lay each bundle into the pan.

Pour the chowdah over the bundles. Cover the dish with aluminum foil and bake for 20 minutes or about an hour until the pasta soaks up all that fabulous broth.

Scoop the bundles onto plates, drizzle with a little EVOO, and call it a dish.

Tasty Tip: When you go to assemble your pasta bundles, set the manicotti into a short glass before you try to stuff the angel hair in. Then "pour" the bundles into the pan.

Turkey Spam Stir Fry

(PAIR IT WITH OPUS ONE AND A HALF)

1 large can turkey Spam

1 bag frozen Chinese vegetables

1 large bunch scallions, rough chop

2-5 jalapeño peppers, seeded, deveined, finely chopped

1 bottle General Tso's sauce

1 can pineapple chunks in natural juice, drained

EVOO

Did Ya Know? People in Hawaii eat more Spam than anyone else in, like, the world! **ALO-HA!**

Get the Spam out of the can—I just pull it out with my fingers. Slice into matchsticks.

Set your largest frying pan or a wok over high heat; hit it with some EVOO and get that smoking hot. Add the scallions, the jalapeños, and the Spam, stir it around until it fries up all crispy and gorgeous—that is why they call it a "stir fry," after all.

Add the veggies and pour on the sauce—I just eyeball it, but it usually takes about a half of the bottle.

Get your rice (did I mention you'd want rice with this? Shoulda read the whole recipe before you started…) and lay it down into a big bowl or platter. Pour the stir fry over the rice, top with the pineapple chunks and a little drizzle of EVOO to add a nice pepper finish to the dish.

WHY NOT WHITE?

VIN TRÉS ORDINAIRE

Chicken Nuggets Salad

(PAIR IT WITH WHY NOT WHITE? VIN TRÉS ORDINAIRE)

1 pound chicken tenders

6 palmfuls seasoned Italian breadcrumbs

1 egg, beaten with a palmful of water

1 bag seasoned fries

1 bag premade salad

1 stick butter, melted

1/2 palmful vinegar

3 cloves garlic, smashed

1/4 palmful dried Italian herbs

S&P (that's salt and pepper)

Parmigiano Reggiano

EVOO

Preheat your oven to 425 degrees, start cooking your fries.

Now get your nuggets on. Salt, pepper, then into the bread crumbs, the eggs, and back to the crumbs. Drop 'em into a big pan with some smokin' hot oil and jump back!

In a super-large bowl, mix together the butter, the vinegar, the garlic and the herbs. Add some salt and pepper. Add in the salad and give that a good toss.

When the fries are all crispy and delicious, drop them into the dressing, give 'em a toss. Add the tenders, hit it again with the S&P (that's salt and pepper), then grate some Parm (that's Parmigiano Reggiano) over the top and give it a good drizzle of EVOO.

Dried Beef Carpaccio

(PAIR IT WITH DUCK, DUCK, GOOSE YA!)

One jar dried beef

One bag ready-to-eat arugala

One jar oil-packed, marinated artichoke hearts

1/2 cup pitted Kalamata olives

1 lemon

EVOO to drizzle on the dish

Pecorino Romano cheese, a big hunk (more on that later in the recipe)

Spread the dried beef in a single layer on a large platter.

Top with the green stuff.

Throw on the artichoke hearts and the olives.

Squeeze the lemon—cut side up!—over the top, drizzle with some EVOO and some shavings of cheese (I use a single-edge razor, but a vegetable peeler will work, too).

Fast Faster Fastest

30-Second Meal

Head on back to page 49 for my Save the Airfare "Sardine-ia" Pasta—no passport needed (hee hee! I swear! I crack myself up!)

15-Second Meal

They don't call 'em "one-stops" for nothin'! While you gas up the car, go inside the mini-mart and grab some ingredients. Use my Brokeback Mountain Pie recipe as inspiration, but do what you can with what you find, because cooking is all about working with what you've got on hand.

Box of instant mashed taters

Can o' mushrooms

Can of beef stew

EVOO

Pour boiling water over taters (word to the wise: do this in a bowl because the box will just dissolve. Trust me on this.)

Pour stew and mushrooms into a baking dish. Top with taters. Drizzle on some EVOO. Pop it in the microwave—set it on HIGH!—for 20 seconds to heat through.

While your shepherd's pie is baking, open up a nice bottle of vino, put your feet up and cuddle up with your sweetie. Who knows? You might forget about dinner altogether!

5-Second Meal

Hit a coupla drive-thrus on the way home and you've got a spread that'll please everyone! Just drop the food down on top of your own dishes (unwrap everything first, of course, heehee!) and I swear no one will know that you let someone else do all the work.

Mea Culpa (That's Italian for "Oops!") and Other Random Thoughts

Hey, Kids! I've Been Thinking…

Y'know, there are times when I stop and reflect on my life and realize just how lucky I really am. The fame. The fortune. (I mean, really, c'mon!) The adoration.

That's all. Just lucky. Of course, I am as perky as a coffee machine in a donut shop. Oh, and I did invent the concept of making a whole meal in no time flat. Did I mention the infectious laugh, the "sassy girl next door" vibe, the goofiness that makes it so easy for people to love me?

So I guess lucky isn't really the right word, is it?

Everybody makes mistakes now and then. Even me.

- Like that time when I had the "wardrobe malfunction" on my daily talk show, *The Rachell Ray Daily Talk Show*. I didn't mean for that to happen, and I apologize to everyone who I flashed. Of course, I don't actually choose my outfits, so that wasn't my fault, exactly….

- Or the times when I forget to wash my hands after handling raw chicken. I know it's a health hazard, people! But I got meals to make, cookbooks to write, a magazine to produce and three TV shows to tape, so sometimes I skip over the little things. Enough with the letters, phone calls and emails; and you can stop sending me soap, already!

- I get that there are some people who confuse my enthusiasm for what my guests are talking about with rude interrupting, but hey, let's remember whose show it is, okay?

- There's been a lot of chatter lately about how I call my viewers "kids." Hey, it's a term of endearment, okay? What should I call them, "ladies and gents"? Whatever.

- Okay, I get that I didn't get famous for my singing voice, but if I want to serenade my ingredients, I'm doing it. Try and stop me.

- And the complaints about the food not looking "pretty" enough? Get. Over. It.

I'm sorry. There, I said it. Now let's move on, people.

Paula Deane

Rach drops in on her friend, Paula Deane, to check out what's in her fridge.

RACHELL RAY: Hey, honey! I came by to see what's in your icebox!

PAULA DEANE: Oh sweet Jesus, why didn't you call first? I'da put on my face, and gotten some vegetables and fruit in. Is that a film crew?

RR: Oh, man! You have a lot of butter and lard and what we used to call "government cheese" in here.

PD: I'm fixin' to make me some fudge. You know, a simple phone call…

RR: Look at this ginormous carton of whipping cream! Now that's a date night if I ever saw one, wink and a nudge. Where do you even find this!

PD: I have my sources. Listen, Rachell, hon…

RR: Y'know, everybody loves you!

PD: I know! Innat somethin'?

RR: Yeah. I mean, even when they make fun of you and that crazy accent of yours, your maniacal cackle, the way you use butter in, like, everything, nobody's really mean about it like they are about me. Why do you think that is?

PD: Well, I don't rightly know, darlin'. But it might have something to do with the fact that I have a somewhat tragic back story and I've overcome things in my life, you know, the bad decisions I've made and what not.

RR: And the food.

PD: There's that. Now Rachell…

RR: Do you think it's also because it's really hard to feel jealous of a woman who's kinda fat and loud and clueless?

PD: Talk about the pot callin' the kettle. You're loud and clueless.

RR: *I know!* But I'm not fat! Because I believe in moderation and eating healthfully.

PD: Now I say this with nothin' but love and best dishes, but have you seen a rear view lately?

RR: I should let you go. But one last question: Which one of my millions of recipes is your favorite?

PD: I don't know how to break this to you, honey, but I actually *know* how to cook, so I don't need any of your so-called "recipes."

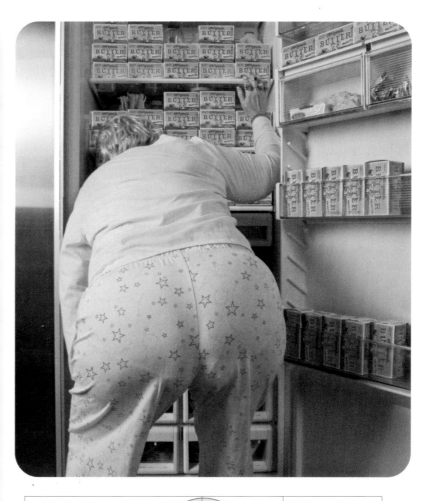

Pop Quiz

1 Paula's fridge is full of:
- **A.** Fruit, vegetables and lean meat
- **B.** Butter
- **C.** Champagne

2 If Paula could invite anyone to dinner, who would it be?

3 What's Paula's favorite food?
- **A.** Butter
- **B.** Butter
- **C.** Butter

A. Guess who?   **B.** Her fave   **C.** Me

Tom "Let's Try It Both Ways" Connor, my friend, "agent provocateur," and book packager par excellence.

My editor, Michele Bidelspach, who completely got every freaking thing about Rachell Ray
and whose guidance helped me fine-tune every freaking page.

Special thanks to Rick Wolff at Grand Central for his support.

This project truly would not have been possible without the great work of The Crew:

Vincenzina "Enza" Civitillo, our darling Rach

Neil "Is This What You Had In Mind?" Swanson
whose photography captured the essense of Rach (and made the food look beautiful, in a disturbing way)

Laura "It's Not Soup, It's Art" Campbell for her inspired design skills

Shannon "You Don't Need A Wig" Hector, hair stylist to the star

Dawn "She Needs More Lipgloss" Collins Hobbs, who brought out the "Rach" in Rach

The DuRay Family

Myles MacVane (Regus Patoff Lesboeuf)

Rita Houston (Honey DuRay-Lesboeuf)

Elaine Osowski (Baby Doucette DuRay)

David Letourneau (Puff Gumpy DuRay-Lesboeuf-DuRay)

Peter Hobbs (DaDa DuRay)

Shannon Hector (Allura Starr Lesboeuf)

Laura Campbell (Sissy Love Lesboeuf-DuRay-Lesboeuf)

Damien Brady (Bubba Lesboeuf-DuRay)

The Scuderia Family

Peter Pastorelli (Big Vito Scuderia)

Laura Fedele (Carmella Scuderia-Francois)

Michael DuMez (Michel "French Connection" Francois)

Dawn Collins Hobbs (Dulcinea Scuderia)

Beatrice Piper Hobbs (Baby Bea)

Sonia Landino (Little Rachell Scuderia)

Vincent "Jimmy" Perrone (Ferrari Scuderia)

Lee Alvarone (Ducatti Scuderia)

Kyle Brady (Little Vito Scuderia)

The author wants to thank everyone else who helped make this book happen, particularly:

Lisa Grenadier for her inspired casting

Jackson Connor

Cassidy Singleton

Donald Robinson

Abby Dodge

Lisa Callahan

Darryl Manning

Thanks also to:

Carol & Mark of Along Came Carol, Fairfield, CT

12-Pack Chris at Consignment Furniture, Westport, CT

Judy Robinson & the Old Wilton Town Hall, Wilton, CT

Anthony's Hairstylists & Wigs, Trumbull, CT

Goodwill Industries, Norwalk, CT

T.J. Maxx

Tinker's Treasures, Bridgeport, CT

The Burger Bar and Bistro, Norwalk, CT

As always, I am completely indebted to Neil Swanson ("the Total Package") for his support,
his encouragement and his unwavering confidence and faith in me.